The Witness Ghost

The Witness Ghost
Tim Bowling

Nightwood Editions

Roberts Creek, B.C.

2003

Nightwood Editions
R.R. #22, 3692 Beach Ave.
Roberts Creek, BC
V0N 2W2, Canada

Edited for the house by Silas White
Typesetting by Carleton Wilson
Interior photographs by Bruce Bowling

We gratefully acknowledge the support of the Canada Council for the Arts and the British Columbia Arts Council for our publishing program.

NATIONAL LIBRARY OF CANADA CATALOGUING IN PUBLICATION DATA

Bowling, Tim, 1964–
 The witness ghost / Tim Bowling.

Poems.
ISBN 0-88971-191-7

I. Title.
PS8553.O9044W57 2003   C811'.54   C2003-910320-X
PR9199.3.B6358W57 2003

Table of Contents

In memory of
Harold (Heck) Bowling
1923–2001

The Witness Ghost

I woke in the dark to your voice
(trickle of creek over rock,
clench of tide around pile).
We left in the dark, the old way,
down the lampless, houseless block,
past the row of wild cherries,
the crunch of our boots on gravel
like the drawn-out growl
of an old dog who doesn't really
mean it. And when the blossoms
touched my cheek, I understood
you had turned back to kiss me
without turning. I went into
those kisses like a bride.

There wasn't any light, though the stars
shone. It was as if someone
looked at us without seeing us;
we could have waved our arms
and never raised a blink. Half-
asleep, I lulled in your easy wake
along the wind-scoured parapet of dyke
down the gangway to the mossy wharf.
A mast chain shivered as we left the planks.

After you had warmed up the boat,
I stood aside and watched you choose
to steer from the cabin not the deck
because a spider in the night
had attached a strand of web
to a spoke. I almost heard you sigh
for the ruin you'd have to make
later, when the dictates of your work
lorded over gentleness, as if
you had to spare a life for those
you planned to take—a reverse sacrifice.

The river trembled, sheened to silk.
Heavy in the damp, the musk
of mud and creosote. Distantly,
a coal train cried, leading
its black pod a little closer
to the kelp. I woke
further. At the towhead,
beside an island of rushes
slightly rising and falling
like the roped chest of Gulliver,
I saw the little throw of lights
up Grouse Mountain, in North Vancouver
where you'd been a boy, splashing
truant in creeks so silver that, whenever
you moved your body, even to kill,
something essential had been smithied,
struck from fire.

The corks rolled off the drum.
You steered across the channel
from the stern. I stood
beside the doomed cathedral
on the deck, my heart
still as the unsuspecting spider.
For ten minutes, we strained
to hear a salmon hit the net.

Then we picked up. Closer,
I watched you hang above
the ripping silk. An urgent whisper
and I came beside you, on rubbery
tiptoe, staring into the drip of black.
Slowly, you bunched in your hands
the web as soft as muddied lace.
We bent like two sunflowers
seeking the earth's internal light.

Shhh. The unending caution
of the breeze. Your lips
had become the vessel of the race.
In your hands, the will to strike.
In your eyes, the wonder that you would.
I hunched into the sudden shadow
of your shoulders, gaping like a baby owl.

Something big was down there. You held
a single mesh between thumb and forefinger
and traced its tooth-snagged geometric
on the air, careful inch by inch. Then angled
the hook of the gaff, prepared to strike.
In the invisible, acrid clots of exhaust,
I held my bones and heartbeat in,
stifled a cough.

The downward arc dipped
in the black before it pierced
the skull in the fatal crush,
striking up from under
at the gill. You rarely missed
and knocked it loose, or stuck
the hook in the valued flesh.
A painter's skill—you must
have traced the pattern of death
ten thousand times
in the roiling dark
until even your sleep was etched
with crossing lines so thick
they came to mimic
the grains in a woodcut.

And I was the spider who watched.
I was the pupil in the crystal,
widening, my black into the black
of the earth, that has to turn and kill
whatever's formed from the guts
of the self—nothing gentle
in the fall of a blossom
onto a street black
as the lid of a coffin,
or in a bubble of black froth
at the torn jaw of a salmon,
nothing gentle in an art that
traces out lines only to turn
and stuff its own creation
in its mouth.

Yet I woke this morning,
and will always wake,
to your voice
and the hopeless task
of replication,
to string along the web
without breaking
the first, struck silver
of dew, and listen for
the dying-as-it's-born
echoing afterclang of hush.

Annual Drive to Pick Up the New Net at the Cannery

It is too late to start
for destinations not of the heart.

– R.S. Thomas

Just dusk. Our father's hardtopped, bubble-shaped,
lime Ford with the unwhite whitewalls
coughed, spluttered, coughed, and almost died
backing out of our gravel drive, slosh-puddled
with the gusting rains that almost never stopped.
In-between season, not winter and not spring.
In-between time, the day in shivers, the moon's
voluptuary fullness made porthole proscription.

But we were the fathom the mind of God was watching.

My sister and I cleared the damp, fallen autumn
of Richie Rich, Uncle Scrooge, and Archie comic books
from the back seat's stippled vinyl, and hunched
our shoulders as we perched and peered
out of our respective window's private pier glass
alive with mostly wind-reft and darkening emptiness,
and stole, for comfort, glances at our father's
immanent posture, head still, neck muscles tensed
as if about to rear and swerve at the gnarled deadhead
roiling just under the pavement's slickly running tide.
He hardly ever drove on land. His all-but-wordless
vigil at the steering wheel transformed the black
potato fields to flowing graves where great chinook

tore scales of pewter from their flesh:
butting, prodding, bull-urgent, they knocked
aside the driftwood's knotted arms
and surfaced where wonder lay fallow.

Our father reaped a constant crop of seeing.
Over mote-stubbled acres, the cock-pheasant's head
hooked up like a bloodied gaff. Alerted
by whispered words and a nod, we'd stare
without result until the auburn body
rose and took the faint horizon in a smear
that faded as fast as it appeared. To orient,
I always sought the sharpening edges of the moon
where it owled our slow and singular traffic
along the farmroads to the skinny river road
that followed, in twists, the shack-barnacled
bank of collapsing docks, the shack-planks
and dock-planks the same, a century
of bloodstains sinking in them
as eye colour descends in the genes.

And now a faint list from our driver
and attentiveness to seals. There—there—
in the moonpath, by the boom. But
there's no horizon and no smear, only
darkness settling on darkness, our breath
rushing the winged moon to the glass
on my side, where my sister crowds in,
her long hair still damp with rain,

the whole car suddenly wet, close,
the fields, the moon, the pheasant's head,
the unseen seal. . . we're drifting against
the current, blood in the hard flesh,
the motor of hunger racing, water
streaming past our strained eyes, time
on the breaking heart of the clock,
stars everywhere in our senses, the
musk of absolute accomplishment,
going down, straight into it, crunching
the gravel underneath the blackly arcing
branches off the main flow and bursting
out into almost sightlessness, ourselves
again, in tiny gasps, the rain again,
sharing with us this running, rampant, breathless
downward plunge to the bone in the matrix
of water, not knowing what will survive
of what we know, no guarantee
of moonrise for memory, only
our hearts shredding a small redd
in the creek's marrow,
and the world clawing at it,
our father wordless in last illness,
my sister and I left to the wheel
and the vague bounty of the glass
as we go on, shadow-drivers
haunted by the shine of blood
in each stop, and breathing, breathing hard
to make an ocean from a fathom of the world.

Singing Frank

We sat around our father
as he and I used to sit
around backyard fires
lingering over the last coals
not needing to speak
when suddenly my brother
a living Confederate soldier
in a Mathew Brady tint
asked, "Do you remember
Singing Frank?" and smiled.

Did I? My brother's memory
was longer with his extra decades
and more of the dead walked there.

"Sure," my sister answered.
"He used to sleep it off
in the blackberry bushes
up on the dyke by the cannery."

Over our father's still body
in the huge ward lit like dusk
she returned our brother's smile.

Singing Frank? I strained
for the cracked tune, the scent
of ripe berries and the river
rising to cover its mud. No.
I didn't think I. . .

"Every Saturday night."
My brother's blue eyes gleamed
above his greying beard.
"Wailing away, flat on his back,
empty bottle of Baby Duck in his hand."

"We used to lob rocks at him, remember?"
my sister added, the one ghost
in her doorway that only lingered
on my porch. "Whenever he stopped,
it always made him start again."

What did he sing, brother? Oh,
old songs, *Santa Lucia*, *Good Night Irene*,
that sort of thing. Sister, how
did he sound? Oh, drunk
as a skunk, bad as the toms
in the tall grass, terrible.

They both grinned. "Ezra Hemsworth,"
my brother went on, "used to go up
and take Frankie's clothes off
once he'd passed out
and leave him there in all his glory
for the church ladies picking berries
on Sunday morning to find. Oh my!"
He placed his work-scarred hand
daintily to his mouth. "Oh my!"

We laughed almost without sound
until the tears came, tears
that felt no different than
others we had cried
that took the same path
down our cheeks, engraving it there.

At the head of the bed, our mother
didn't look up from his closed eyes
but something of what we said must
have reached her. She softly sang
her lips almost touching his right ear
"I'll be loving you always, always"—
one of the old songs, uncracked,
rising surely as the river
only to fall again, and rise, like the years,
as we dumbly picked the sweet, black water from our skin.

Last Breath

We knew it was coming, but we didn't know when.
That morning, my two year old, for the first time, said,
"I want to kiss Grandpa," was lifted to your closed eyes.
Down again, he turned quickly at the foot of the bed,
and smiling, waved. A bird smashed through
the glass of my playhouse window.

Then I was alone, speaking to a silence
I would know the rest of my life. Every word
was a struck, damp match, and meant
only that I breathed. Then your middle son
came to vigil at your other side. When
did we look across your body and know?

We knew it was coming, but when it came
we waited our lifetimes for another intake
and harsh exhale. But into the hole
in the glass your being pursued
its flight. We heard a soft break
in our chests—air rushed in like sand.

In the mouth of the river
briefly
a seal surfaced and its eyes were blue.

At the River's Edge

Gently, the nurse offered
the last photograph ever taken
of you (that the staff had taken).
In it, you were old, tired, worn
with the fight of life, your eyes
dull, nowhere. I couldn't bear
the possession, but I kept
the cheap Polaroid in
my coat pocket, and forgot it
all that long first day of loss
until well after midnight
alone on the wharf, the tang
of the lowering tide, the vinegar
and fat of the fish-and-chip shop,
making nostalgic the summer air.

Two of the boats moored nearby
belonged to men you fished beside.
Your voice was layered in those hulls
beneath the mud and brine. I heard
the tone but not the words (and
that's another form of death).
The harbour channel's calm
was like a child's bath, though
obsidian and flowing out.
I wanted a heron to disturb the black,
a sucker to flip and ripple, anything
to focus on beside your final breath.

When I remembered the photo, and pulled it
from my pocket, and peered at it
in the waxpaper moonlight, I knew
the image wasn't you. The spirit
was gone, as if, as Crazy Horse
believed, the camera stole it
and left a blank. And yet
I could not bring myself to destroy again
what Time had just destroyed forever.

My hands shook. Branch and leaf,
I dropped our autumn in the river.

The dead are not buried face-down—
we assume a vision for them
of distances we can't measure.
And I know you're vital
in the whale's eye, sickness
scoured by tide and star,
your look softening as you turn
spindrift under the pulse's roam
or at the land's edge where
the flesh-bound go to wonder.
One image deliberately given
to memory, out of all the images
memory takes from us.

No matter where smoke travels
we know its origin in fire.

I think of your smile
in a hundred years,
an easement
to some unborn spirit's
salt watch-hour.

A Life

In cramped spaces pungent with mildew, earth,
oil and rain—garden sheds, netsheds, the cabins
of two salmon boats: the *Nautilus* and
the *Nola J*—he waited out, even in youth,
the King Lear weather of the coast.
And when he couldn't wait, he went,
bending at the neck
as the sunflowers he loved
now mourn their absent sun.

It is the living, not the final,
stillness I recall,
the absoluteness of the invitation
to the hour. *You're coming,*
so come, his presence said
to October in the downpours
April in the teems,
and he heard the approach
even when it was only
a caterpillar crawling
over a bed of moss.

Once, in a thunderstorm,
neither a child nor a man,
I took a cup of tea

down the narrow sideyard—
of rusted bikes with flattened tires
half-sunk in the brown-bruised apple blossom
and broken wheelbarrows spilling water
like loam over their sides—
to where he sat
behind the dingy fibreglass
of a humble greenhouse
its opacity lost
to the brine-shingling winds.

The rain burbled a froth
in the barrows and eaves
and in the little cup I carried
until heat slopped over to burn
my thumb and forefinger
and I quickened my pace under
the overhang of apple boughs
to the patch of open garden
staked with sawed-off hockey sticks.
There, pausing, I saw
the lightning flash his stillness
through the gauze of fibreglass
once, violently, his black form
sudden in the midday gloom.
Etched, scorched out of wetness,
he seemed the momentary

skeleton of the tiny space
he'd made his refuge. I blinked
and washed another gulp
of milky tea onto my hand,
then squelched across the earth
to find him calmly smoking
in the closeness, as if
he didn't know, or couldn't
find a way to stop,
the image that the father
has to make
to free the son.

I don't mean anything except necessity
when I say that death is freedom—
to accept, like Lear, your nakedness,
the mildew, the husks of flies
in the corners of cramped spaces
where you set your posture
to the world, the cane-tap
of the blind rain at your thought.

It was all water and murmur
at the source, my loved, my lost stillness,
and water and murmur in the first
days without you. Now
I await the fire of a near hour
to frame me for my child.

After a Death

It's the most amazing thing. I can move
my body towards others on the busy streets
of any city, and they will adjust. I can speak
to anyone—this pretty girl beside me in the café
where I write, that pox-scarred man in the crosswalk
hunched into his collar—and they will look
in my direction, even respond in kind.

There can be little doubt: I must be alive.
As Samuel Johnson refuted Bishop Berkeley
by kicking a stone to prove that matter exists,
I lean towards flesh to hear my heartbeat,
and look into eyes to see the coming year.
It is perhaps an easy thing to say
the downed leaf does not negate the tree,
but we live by isolating the fall of each life,
and must attend the tracery of veins
in absence to find again the warm embrace.

One day we blend back into the current
and move for the one who needs our shift
and respond to the one who longs for voice.

But now, and for as long as necessary,
I will prove by asking others to exist
that I have not gone with you into death.

Dead Is the Word that Belonged to Others

Dead is the word that belonged to others,
grandparents, the poker buddies who burst
arteries crossing barnyards, famous Americans
waving out of open convertibles. Now it's yours.
I woke last night to hear you say, *I'm dead, Tim,*
simply, as if speaking of another gaffed fish
in your thirty years of work. And you said
nothing else. I lay there with the new word.
It was so young I wanted to protect it,
for you and all your sudden family, to keep it
unsullied by useage, out of the papers, off
the wet mouths of the living who know nothing
of the little doors in the letters they mouth.
But I felt the stone harden in the four pillars.
The word became a stillborn swaddled
in your skin that I'll never touch again.

Dead. It always belonged to others.
Now the knell of its saying is yours,
the weight of its carriage, mine. And ours.

The Grieving Place

If you're human, you'll have to go there,
and you'll take the unexpected
with you, like an ant that,
dragging a crumb of bread,
carries the baker's pain.

But the place will be yours: no one
can join you in it, no more than
a dream can be dreamed
in separate bodies.
Allow that loneliness:
it is the gift the dead give
to make our community
with the animate in stone
boundless.

I will go to my grieving place
and find the brittle twine
of old summers cobwebbing
the shadows, and the meshes
of young springs like shocked grain
on the planks. There will be
the smell of low tide and ripe
blackberries and musty books.

And there will be a feeling
I cannot explain
except to say, here is
a glass float from Japan,
the size of a classroom globe,
bluish-green, crystalled as a starry night,
bearing inside the birth-cry of a whale
and an old widow's year of salt;
and here is the one loose pearl
of roe stripped from a salmon,
red as only August is red,
slippery as a seal's tear,
the currency a leaf pays
to be allowed to die.
Between the float and the egg
my body will be still
and the thought and the breath
that is mine
will fill first the large
and then the small roundness
exchanging in the long hours
tidally
salt and blood,
water and light.

And when I rise
and break into
my home waters, those
riverbanks of weeping
willows, mossy sheds,
and listing houses,
the full moon that lights
the Asian widow's way
accompanies my stream,
while, hanging from the blackberry bushes,
dew-slickened, throbbed
with the foretaste of falling,
quickened by the moon,
the split, abundant roe of summer shines.

How the World Looks, After a Death

The dark is the dark inside a dead whale.
One morning, when the blubber's rotted off,
you're left with houses, wharves, streets,
yawning gulls, dog shadows, and stench—
that's how living builds a town of grief.

You can sleep a thousand miles away
yet walk there, picking stray gobbets
out of the overcast, you can extend
a rung-gapped wooden ladder far into the middle
of a clustered bush of blackberries
and climb out over the rich abyss
of your own grave and, prickled
to the forearms, lie on your back
under the terrible scratches of the stars
on the underlid of being and cry until
you transform the dyke to a Greek chorus
of dogs. You can search in vain forever
for the scrimshaw on the one raindrop
that will be your map through the jaw-gates.

I can tell you what it's like,
but you already know, or will,
or it won't be the same for you at all.
Still, if words can be true, these are:

I come from a small town by a river.
My father, a kind man, is dead there.
I live in a northern city now, but I hear
the hollow whalebeat of a shunted boxcar
echoing across yards of ash and cinder.
It's the sound of the street I'm walking down
where the sky's a bruise and the gulls yawn
from atop the steeples and lampposts of bone.

But ahead I scent the creek of clear water
where, thigh-braced to the rush of cold,
the hunger-to-be is steadily raking
with its claws
fierce tears out of the eyes of God.

I Prefer a Single Light

I prefer a single light
to read by when my wife
and children are asleep,
so that when I look up
from the communal page,
there's the roaming weight
of dark against the glass,
heavy in the leafless trees. I prefer
my solitude black and searching,
the dead craning at the bright edges
to peer over my shoulders, silence
the mumming of the language
they have lost. I prefer to be
driftwood on the blood of spirit
that doesn't ebb.

The single light has long been mine.
Porchlight that holds the mother's worry
like a draining moth
Sternlight that welds the father's hunger
to the salmon's death
Streetlight that frames the child's body
like a branch of autumn leaves

And the matchlight's shivering drop of blood.

These too are not diffuse, but one.
The child on the corner drifts to the sea.
The mother walks from the porch to the corner.
The father eyes the black catch of the page.

And I go on with the rest of the living,
striking my matches off the bone.

Last Time Home, Late Spring

The red comes into the apples and cherries
and the gills and the humps of the salmon
at almost the same rate
it leaves the sky and the planks of barns,
comes into the skin of the child
as it leaves the skin of the old.
Where life drains away, life returns.

The blood of the whole of history
seeps into the ground and the rivers
and spots the pages of the texts:
is it possible it grows nothing, now,
but more of the same waste of itself?

I have chosen the dappled coolness
of a weeping willow
to stretch myself under.
The shadow trembles
as if about to birth
a killer whale. Nearby,
on a little wharf,
the tail of a spring salmon
like a fan of night sky
sticks up from a metal bucket,
and above a cluttered yard
three white T-shirts
dry on a clothesline

moving slightly
as if three chests
breathed in them.

I think I will believe
in the colour of the hidden flesh
a while longer, and rise,
as a man rises, tipping
the red a little closer
to the surface of life.

West Coast

The dark is wet, warm, and scented.
The teabag of a town steeps in it.
Thinly, moonlight is stirred in.
In the empty harbour
a salmon lifts and turns over,
the arc of a pewter spoon.

Even the waking are sleeping.
What has died, or otherwise
been lost, is found. Such as

the man in silence, smoking
off the stern of a salmon boat
as if it were a porch hung
over a visible, flowing fragrance.
For forty years he has watched
summer's dusk become its night,
imperceptibly a winter pelt
grows over the bones of an animal.
He has stood in the red benedictions
of place and been moved at variable speed
between the salt and mud hollows
between youth and the age he has come to,
which is the age of knowing that what moves him
is a greatness inarticulate, an unsaying,
each word cancelled by the last breath
of the life sprawled silver at his boots.

A star falls timed to the dousing of his cigarette.
The sizzle is of the vast going into the deep.
What the man thinks is what love and work
have taught; what he feels is the weight
of flesh assimilated into the order
of loss. The river takes him down,
a dark arm lowered
to place a child in the grass.

How can Time employ its suffering here?
The fishnets hang like bridal veils
off the moon,
the corn in the fields
competes with the farmers' sons
for quickest leaps in height,
and the silt building in the river
is the song building in the throats
of the blackbirds in the rushes.

It matters less
that the motion
of the muscle in the arms
of the man as he bends
to his net is savage and mortal,
that the muscle pulls from the river
as the beak of the eagle
pulls from the guts of the salmon.

It matters less
how the drawn smoke spreads
through the body
in a map without rivers,
mountains or towns,
or how the unsaying passes
to those who, grieving,
try harder to say.

Something about those mouths without air.
Something about that flesh growing stiff.
Something about grains of salt in the dusk
and dusk in the flowing of the river.

Yet stay. Waking, we can be our dream
a while longer. It is in the nature
of wanting that a town steeps
never to be poured
into the cup of its ashes
and that the loose-moored skiffs
against the pilings
knock out the rhythms
of a heartbeat still.

The Harvest

A man and a boy on a river
in a boat drifting rapidly to sea.
They labour together in the stern,
salmon fluent at their gumboot tops,
others flopping in across the rollers,
hanging, thrashing, in the meshes.
Over the island poplars
the tiny moon tenses
at every tug on the web,
creeps its white sack forward.

Late August. The corn has been cut
in the fields they drift past. The scent
of cut peas is on the wind, cut hay.
The salmon's mouths open and close,
open and close, like quick wounds.
The man and the boy drift faster.
At their legs, the sickles cut.
Decorously. As a caretaker cuts
the grass of the unvisited graves.
Almost without sound.

The boy fell first, too many
years ago to count.

And the man with the nimble fingers
who spoke always with a deer's look?

Three months ago this day,
the river struck his gold.

Since July

How much silver in the heron's bill and
how many storms builded to break and
how many cries of the coal trains going down to the sea?

Between my eyes and the stars, darkness.
Invisible, the exposed nerves of the elm trees.
Your boat in memory is a deathbed.
I'm forever in its wake.

It can't be that spiderwebs are torn only
by escaping prey, or by the running boy
who pulls the gauze from his mouth
briefly noting it, as we note days;
sometimes the wind just takes them
down, the minor scaffolding of hours
over the great cathedral where the belltower
keeps no bell.

Because I watched the last seconds
of you pass in a series of sheer dissolutions
as if your face were made of a finery
equal to what the skill of nature weaves,
and my hands went up to stroke your brow
and to pull the gauze from my own mouth
at the same time: when your breath stopped,
though the heron had to swallow
and the coal to go down to the sea,
all the gentlest frames of my life gave way.

Anniversary

Woodsmoke. Rough veins of the tomb rock.
Over Ladner whose marshy ground
can only grave a salmon or a dog,
whose only promontory, apart from smoke,
is the black crag of a scarred whale
on the barnacles. No depth, no height.
And the mountains slay distance,
the overcast hunches every back.
The prickles of the blackberry
clench to fists. Mute,
the trumpets of the morning glory.

I smear the mosquito on my palm
to wear your blood, the endless cedar
smutch of the possible. But hope is bad science.
A mosquito lives a few hours
and you've been dead a year.

Shirtless in your garden, I dig
the earth over, crunching the soft gravel
of fish you caught, dogs
who lay at your feet, came
at your whistle. The mosquitoes
thick as smoke. I swat and kill,
scorched by a hundred points of fire

cold at the source. Cold, recent,
the blood I wear is my own.

It So Happened

It so happened that I stayed awake
in a still house sodden with the moon's
light and heard my children cry out,
briefly, in disturbed dreams,
almost at once in their rooms
separated by a long hallway
of scuffed wood. The darkness
around the moon's light
flowed swiftly as a river
around the creaking
of two anchor chains.

It so happened my father was ashes
a month, and his death
was theirs too in the calm hours
and I couldn't leave it alone,
the weight of the drag under
the flow. Earlier, I had made
a woman cry with this philosophy,
that any embodied joy
must end in ash, a thought
no mother can pursue, or should:
what does the end of bone matter
to each remade instant's remade gesture?

It so happened that the silence
after the simultaneous cries
shook me more than the fact
of fear and pain a father
cannot salve, for I knew
the motion of the bones
inside the ash:
his hands reset the chains
and they did not creak again
because the tear my darkness
brought to her skin
it so happens
oils the future's interstitial sleep.

We Die Many Times Before We Die

On the coast where I was born
there's a phone booth by the government wharf,
up on the gravel dyke, by blackberry bushes,
shrouded in salmon-stink, brine, and
those sodden pea-coats the sky always wears
over waters forever tucking kelp and cedar
up to their chins. The scaled and bloodied gangways
lie level, or tilt almost vertically according to tide,
and there's a sad angle of crucifixion
to the wood as the moon pulls it,
and your rain-droned shoulders, up,
with a single scale in your palm to make a call.

Because no one ever calls this blurry glass,
the heart must be active when it enters,
seven digits in the mind like the points in a constellation
and the voice in the throat so much silver
poised to re-enter familiar waters.

You can almost believe in reaching the dead.
They are almost where they always were,
on lamplit chesterfields reading evening papers,
by kitchen sinks, in bedrooms, turning
the earth, at the living's unceasing, ordinary vespers.
Wait for me, you say, wringing the flow of the world
from your hands, I'll be home soon,
as soon as I clean the plugs of these stars

as soon as I mend the web of this air
as soon as the rain stops telling me
in deathbed whispers
no one's really there, or ever will be there.

And the ringing that persists
when we return to the weather
is only the blood in the body
of the old life
lifted slowly
on its trodden cross.

Chisholm Street to Georgia

As if sentient, the blossoms on the salt breeze
come with me as I walk the old streets,
bearing the weight of missing you
as we once bore the fresh salmon
for private sales in potato sacks
across the dyke, and home, to lay
their blood-sticky silver in
the starshine and ripe pear light.
Over the shoulders, at the crossbeam,
where the past prefers to settle
until born again as myth. I almost expect
the blossoms to whisper *Wrong way*,
or *Go slower*, or, suddenly, in a child's voice,
It's okay, I can make it, it's not too heavy.

How much that dead weight shifted!
As if the souls had decided to exit
the cage of bone and gill at last
only to find the dust of an old yield,
heavy as the blood of a suicide,
mantling flight. It seemed
our muscles worked outside our flesh
until we reached the gravel drive
and let the burlap fibres drop
from our abraded grips. And when
we slept, the motion of the river
and the motion of the dead gave

a sliding surface to our dreams:
the keys, and not the fingers
of the pianist, moved.

Now I wear the salted blossom cape
into the corner streetlamp glow
and the last half-block of silence
before I reach the house
of your widow's solitude. What
do the blossoms whisper of the animate
in memory? The breeze that bears
the answer bears my body home
along the old street, this crossbeam
of the earth we shared. Weight
of the child and man, weight
of the planet the same. When
I lay the cold scales down
at the side of the house
it is my skin that feels
the probing hunger of the stars and wasps.

You Fathered the Rain

You fathered the rain
and wherever it touches me
Vancouver, Edmonton, Galway-
by-the-sea, I feel
my brother's hand.
Even when
in cold and dark
he strikes the waters
a hundred thousand
hissing tongs, I am not
cast out, but stand
secure in coming gentleness.

You fathered the rain
where the Coast Mountains
tremble a heron's powdery blue
on the sawdusted eddies
and dogs with backs
of doused ashes
whimper at the end
of the moon's brittle chain.

Any day can be your child.

How can I not love them more,
now you are not here
to love them? I owe you this,
always, all places, Vancouver,
Edmonton, Galway-by-the-sea.
Cells of the life we are—downpour!

The Promise

I am going to start remembering silence,
the silence
after the fisherman strips the roe from the sockeye
after the young girl tears the page from the diary
after the killer whales crash their headstones under
then breech in glistening spadefuls of earth

when the fisherman holds the cold cloth of life in his hand
when the young girl feels the flesh pull away from her spine
when the whales wash into the sea like ink.

In the false dark of man
the dark of the midday barn
I am going to remember the silence
after your last breath
when the world was the ball of an eye
that couldn't feel its tear

and in that memory
I won't see anything
except my children making friends with the grass.

Old Song

They had to cut the smoke out of the smokehouses.
Only in the eyes of seals, the salmon's death.
It was too soon for me, but I lived.
It was too soon for you, but where's your life?

The grunt and slobber of the bruin-faced world,
peremptory, in the black heart of the hive,
stole the downward shove on my shoulderbones.
But it had to go somewhere, that force
I see as the dark between stars. Why not
into the drive of the foot on the shovel-blade
that prepares our matter for the earth?

The robin at the pit without piercing the flesh.
They had to rip into the clouds for the rain.
It was too soon for me, but I lived.
It was too soon for you, but where's your life?

If there's a God, he's masked in blossom
and his hands are slippery with river mud
and his light is as harsh to you as this world's
once was to me. Now your light is stolen
as the last dark of the womb. The same theft
except. . . no, not the same. Untimely
for the living can be timely for the dead.

Out of the killer whale's song, the cry of the gull.
They had to gut the fisherman's hands for the fish.
It was too soon for me, and I live.
The world's Caesarean when we grieve.

Explanation for the Flight of the Great Blue Heron

I recall the moonless night
a dozen seals surfaced
soundlessly
around our boat
and we drifted a moment
in the graveyard of an English rectory
looking for our family name
on those sloped, shoulderless, rain-black stones.

We couldn't find our line in those eyes
and I couldn't find it in the English
years later when I stood alone
in the flow of the crowded shambles
whose names are lifted from the legacy
of slaughterhouses. That trip, just arrived,
jet-lagged, hallucinating in a churchyard
on a hill in Lewes, I could have been adrift
among the curious seals. Homesick,
I came back to where a single sturgeon
out of the depths of the Fraser
might well have been
older than the stamp
in the book of our bloodline's
passage. And back, as well,
without you now, always,
to where the great blue heron
flies over the marsh
carrying our wet name
on two stone slabs to the cemetery.

Remembrance

We used to blacken the windows, wreathe black
the door. Now the children of the dead grieve
privately in metaphor. Elegy is the wheels
spinning on the bicycle of the capped boy
who brings the yellow telegram telling
of the sons who fell in the wars.
The neighbourhood knew the pain.
We blackened the windows, blackly
wreathed the door. Now the blood
has drained from the poppy
we've worn for eighty years.
I refuse that hollow wreath.
I won't be that rotten door.
Better to go and hear
the cattle screaming in the abbatoirs.
Afraid to die, afraid to live:
these are the same fears.

Elegy is the sound of windfall pears
hitting the wet grass. And we die
like this; living, we die like this,
mute at the little grief-windows
of the flesh.

Nickname

Slices under three fingernails
I spent the morning gutting
pumpkins for your grandchildren
who want to be, by turns,
a witch, a pirate, a burglar
(who, as Dashiell says, sneaks
into your house to steal your
cans of beans). And suddenly,
as if he could see the boy I was
and the father you were—and
maybe he could—a ghost!
Not a surprising choice, of course,
but still it took me unaware.
I'd been thinking of us by rote
as I scraped the stringy insides
from each skull, how many years
I watched you with the knife
design the face of jagged teeth
and fix the candle in its wax
onto the upturned lid of a Mason jar.
Such ease, and I always smiled to think
how little of it I possessed, clenching
my jaw as another triangular eye
wandered out of shape. Well,
your grandson wants to be a ghost,
and the word became a sudden trigger
for memory, as most words are,

having been spoken more often
by the dead than the living. I recalled,
looking down at the orange-smeared
newspapers on the kitchen tiles,
how every summer you were printed
up in the local weekly as a "ghost"
because, though on the roster,
you never attended the charity game
between the women's softball champs
and the Pioneer Oldtimers
(mostly fishermen and farmers).
Too shy, I guess, or insecure
about your skill (though no one's
hand and eye were better matched
to hit a rising pitch or snag
a wicked liner). I never asked.
I always knew the public sphere
was not your favoured place.
And so they called you "Ghost"
and put you on the roster
and played the game, those
older, married men
flirting with the girl at short
as she tried to make the tag,
and after a while, no one
even noticed the joke,
though it always ran, until
the pioneers became too old
to bend for grounders.

And now you are a ghost
and even the private sphere
of the world is lost to you.
And here I am
pain and blood under my nails
because I scraped the pumpkins
with my fingers, and the dewed
pulp sliced sharp as any blade.
You would have used a spoon.
You would have carved a neater face.
Well, what does any of this mean
except I loved you and you're gone?

Tonight,
in the sodden pumpkin fields of Ladner
frost grizzles the unharvested fruit
where it lies unchosen, unfaced,
scattered like roe out of a black gash
in the belly of the river.
Dante would have sought his answer
of a shade, Tennyson of a spirit,
and I have had occasion to address the soul.
I have cleaned the guts off the type
of the flattened paper and rearranged it
to satisfy in this public way
some private need I can't begin to understand
except to know, without you,
there's a cut that cannot heal
and I feel it when I hold the pen.

My heart is gnawed at by the frost.
I wear beneath every expression
this little smile of loss.
Pain and blood. Pain in blood.
Where are you, reluctant teammate,
shy man, immaculate hand and eye?

I ask, and cut the sweated bedsheet
to make my child's ghost.

Now It Is the World's Turn to Die

Now it is the world's turn to die,
the trees unfleshing, the salmon
mushroom-soft, red-pulping
their birth waters, the sun rolling
away on jaundiced sheets.

All along the home river
in the tattered cottonwoods
the heads of bald eagles
like elbows poked through
frayed brown coatsleeves,
and a skiff too small to be named
for a woman or a star
tugging at its oily half-hitch
in the yacht shadows.

Surrounding, in the cornfields,
the gold chaff is dull, and dulled
further by the harvested pumpkins
heaped pyramidal, tight as roe.
On the shoreline, empty crab shells,
ochre bloodspots,
and the brittle eyes still gazing ahead
as if to find the tiny brains
somewhere in the salt, dark wash—
a lab, unleashed, crunches them blind,
making a dry echo for the distant surf.

The world dies seeing
not remembering.
The windfall apple is unbitten
and the bruise is a new heart,
one quiet beat for the dew,
as your death bends my body
more often over my children,
one arm a scythe
and the other a net—
what the day cuts
it will also seek to hold.

Let us look through the bruise
Let us listen through the dark
Let us taste how the flesh
is sweetened by the fall

Then let us fall in the wet grasses
wide-eyed
to the detailed spreading
of the winter nights over us.

Going Back

The land's more sensitive now.
A spiderweb bleeds when it's broken;
when a rock is thrown in the river,
there's a cry of pain. And when
the sun sets, it goes down
like a burning stone being lowered
by a man with no skin on his hands.

Why should we leave any differently than the day?
Why should what we build survive
when the spider's gut-creation breaks?

Of course the river cries at its changes.
Of course the light bleeds, ending.

And even though, born of this air,
I will make again in the dawn's wet
webs heavy as cream,
I will not be blinded
by the making.

Even the web that survives,
by autumn
is brittle and cracked
and leaving the world
like spent semen.

Written in the Frost on an Old Wharf

My father who, in youth,   could shoot a pheasant
could not shoot a deer

in life,   who stopped ten thousand salmon
cannot stop the years

in youth,   who could stand in rain
and be the rain and rainlessness

in life,   who lived through every weather
cannot live through death

in youth,   in youth,
the sad eyes of the deer
blinking through the rain

in life,   in life,
the blue eyes of my father
will not be again.

In the Middle of the First Winter

He opened doors softly,
closed them the same. All my home years
this little latch-click in the blood
on the ways out, the ways in,
our well-brined door a gill
of the summer night at rest
in its shallows, breathing
to store the energy
for the last climb into Fall,
breathing the ferment of cherries
that maddened the robin's song
and the oil of the blackberries
on the tongues of young girls
whose arms flashed bronze
in a moonlight that trembled
with salmon fins.

On the river,
by the slow pistons of seal-rise
above the scud of whales
where the islands smelled
of salt and honeysuckle
my father softly closed
his cabin door, opened
it the same. In my bed
my body felt the latches
and the moon gilling

even in its grave. When you open
and when you close
you stand always at a threshold
to be crossed, with a bride,
a stillborn baby, silver
hooked in your fingers and
bleeding on the braided rugs,
done with breath, you stand
with eyelids fluttering
the length of your body
and the dark another door
whelped of mud and meltwater
the hang of flesh and fire
on your shoulder joints,
you went softly, Father, and I,
who bear the same river,
hear on this frozen air,
the crickets clicking latches
on all our summers till we die.

Crab Traps in Snowfall

I walk out to see them again
stacked on the gravel dyke
near the ochred oil drums
and collapsing boatworks,
wound black wires in the swirl of flakes,
empty of victims but inviting death
as if still lying on the ocean floor,
blurred in ceaseless tides of salt.

My limbs are wrack and drift.
Loss means holding blood in charred wires
that flared when you were here.
Now my body refuses the horizon
any light. Can it be we laughed
beside this river, driving west
towards the Gulf, where phosphor
in the salmon-nets is *fire in the water?*

Words are the same impossibility—
they burn in the wrong element
for pain. I have walked out
to where the pliered skeletons
endure the storm. What scuttles,
rasps, rakes the silence
is the last thought in the brain
that knows it will die in water,
home but still death's element.

All the torn drafts of the years
we wander through. And the red claw
charging subtly the burnt wires.

Reach for me across the bottom of the sea.
The true form. Lost father. *Fire in the water.*

Pushing the Stroller in -25

For the first time in months
the moon is whiter than the snow-
bleached hasp of seal skull
gnawed by the blue wash
of the late-day sky. Everything
is so fragile now,
the blades of grass that make
the ribcages of the creatures
we're not subtle enough to name
crushed under this. . . wanting,
this longing for the clean planet
on the other side of silence.

The few people who pass us
move like the stems of delicate flowers
being arranged in a vase of cut crystal.
Above, the elms' black branches
spread out, mounted wingbones
of owls in flight. I wait
for their gun-crack of motion.

All's a cruel taxidermy of absence.
Yet I feel a human whisper
could turn the earth.

I can't breathe it. My son,
swaddled, only his eyes visible,
says, "Look, Papa, the moon.
And it isn't even the dark time."

A Cold Night. Some Snow.

A cold night. Some snow.
Enough to lay salmon skeletons
on the evergreen boughs.

Russian music, Japanese poetry, Canadian winter.
It might as well be
Japanese music, Canadian poetry, Russian winter.
Nothing and nowhere human consoles.

And the non-human returns
empty-clawed
to the bones in the trees.

All night I hear a hunger I can understand
grinding its wings on the edge of a scream.

A Christmas Card to Strangers

At least 365 times this past year
I was aware of days. Of
the thousand-plus changes
of tide, I noted very few.
In August, I wrote of the setting sun,
"It is a pool in which the world
washes the blood off its hands."
With my wife, I made a child.
Late in the year (was it November?)
I was briefly nostalgic
for the Dewey Decimal System
and dreamed of Miss Brokenshea
the tiny Japanese substitute teacher
who came and went through all the years
of my childhood
like a polished shell
the sea and earth competed for.
My father, whom I loved
more than any man, died.
I wrote several poems for him.
I put my ear to my wife's stomach
to hear his footsteps returning.
I let my two children, like oars,
pull me to where I needed to be.
Mostly, I didn't mind the rain.
It seemed, as always,
too gentle for this world.

Acknowledgements

I wish to thank the poetry jury of the 2001–2002 Canada Council competition for awarding me a grant to work on this book.

Special thanks to Joan Harcourt at *Queen's Quarterly* for her longstanding interest in my writing, and to everyone at Nightwood (especially Silas White and Marisa Alps) for their enthusiasm and kindness.

"The Grieving Place" and "West Coast" previously appeared in *Event*.